uncomfortable music

barracuda guarisco

containment:

street crustaceans
5
even when you fail to inspire
7
philosophy with a side of peas
8
the new year comes with a bright light
9
i'm so used to memes i kept looking for the joke
10
can you be the new mtv
11
coronavirus book deal
12
i don't even know who you are
14
notes from the bunker / uncomfortable music
15
this guy stares at me like he's put my unit # on the list of places to
hit when the riots start
16
remote desktop connections
17
gov. inslee calls me out for going outside barefoot
18
how is life on the new obverse
19
wasting the soft moon on absurdity
20
diaries for everyone
21

street crustaceans

the soft noisy needle of microsleep
pings operant conditioning

an organism, breathing mute its
holy computation of the gleaming
animated record veiled in virga
veiled in existential olympics

we are grown and formed
inside peanut shells

we emerge from wicker,
mimicking daredevil

cacoethes

we live in tandem with death
lend it discussion, representation

without us death is nothing
though living could go without

and, no, i don't like that answer,
i don't like that answer

we, like the mon calamari,
must acknowledge the probability

what's been sold as a conference
is more or less a quarantine

is more or less a guillotine

now it's a detoxifying staycation
where self-service, i'm told,

will shock-awake enough
battle cells and hollywood

euphoria to drown

this fuck-ass march madness

of pending transactions
and one-time corporate

courtesies

even when you fail you inspire

is that your oatmeal slug
fictionalized peach

nibble clogging the disposal?

reaching is pretty much
sponge death post-

mafia scowls

yet here we are kiddoz
we popped sickle cellular

we sunrised

we sunrised

& had a day

philosophy with a side of peas

grattered au gratin in the hot seat
of participation

just shouting clever observations
but nobody is laughing due
to my monotone voice
& poor timing

why did you choose to share that?

because i wanted to let them know

i was paying attn

the new year comes with a bright light

the club scene outside is screaming
and i cannot pinpoint a single,
distinguishing characteristic—

it's just cats on ice

another tornado we stop to film,
pushing back the runtime,

blasting iowa by slipknot,
we present the offensive finger

as it draws closer,
we believe we've been making friends

i'm so used to memes i kept looking for the joke

she's posted the meal she cooked
for her man,

but where is the 9 year old
who disappeared

using a cream that makes you ten years younger?

look at your life, son

shake it for gordon ramsay.
will he throw it? will gordon ramsay

fucking beat you with it?

look at you, getting beaten
by your own life, son

the great suspicion has created a great delay

can you be the new mtv

i'll be the astronaut on the moon,
watching you on television
bouncing in the blue sand

moon gumby offers me
a little tea as a treat for my labor

i waive my right to it
because spending time
with you is incredibly special
& i don't want to lose it in the fog

coronavirus book deal

silver rock
& mercury water
everything else is cardboard
crayon drawings of
canyons,
differential renditions of dawn
& dusk;
dungeons & dragons
& dungeness
crabs
why not throw a little moose
into the mix, call 'em
a viking camel
it's funny how one may project
and another may perceive
or categorize what's heartfelt
funny as in humorous,
funny as in strange
i've become so familiar
and accepting of this body
yet feedback has placed detail
on what is misshapen,
prizing it a clinical name
selling it or spinning it
as something prestigious
though i know it's chronic,

not dope, though,

no, not dope

i mean chronic

like i'm stuck

with this shit

my entire life

i don't even know who you are

scissor me up presidential
& rebellious

you know, when the hair is slick
& combed all uniform

w/ a wet-look provided
by poor hygiene

like an open house
at a trailer park

john mulaney is there
he is telling you how

he regularly smelled cocaine

up his nose with the tenacity
of joe biden

he apologizes for the insensitivity of the joke
he doesn't even know who you are

**notes from the bunker /
uncomfortable music**

_____ delivered to our door
varnished in purell

we crawl back into our
mess of a duvet

where only one %
make it to salami

plans for today strike whips
against the navigation of our hands

plans for today:
a home without hands

a piece of pizza floats
by string

safety culminated;
free to ingest, sans serif =

the transferable properties
of mere death's eastwind

calculated bites, extracted
w/ surgical need

i'm fixated on the
ozymandias, incubated

allowing the maximum passage
for a perfect storm

a year-cut night
of pets 2

have you seen it?
it's an animated feature

**this guy stares at me like he's put my unit #
on the list of places to hit when the riots start**

in all the pandemics in all of history, larry the
cable
guy—   who i always confuse for
guy fieri—

suddenly is our voice of reason

whatta abysmal baptismal of the
apocalypse residency —

undone like a kavanaugh tantrum,
i'm a journalist, talk show host;
i'm a midnight toker

check your mail for the invite
to my especially curated

live from the bunker &
trademarked yikes

i'm a cartoon mouse
on this side of my
blacked out
screen   napping among the scented flowers

dreaming of all the different colors
    i can dye my hair, but i must remain conservative

certain styles if not most styles do not look good
(on me)

when it's the end of the world you don't need
    that kind of shade

remote desktop connections

rising otter perches like fondant
on its icy ramp, its island; the cake

ignorant of the existence of a cherry's

upgrade // this is the maglite day eruption

blinding your eyes; using your newborn eyes,
slitted to sharpen the measures of precaution

when there's a human voice
    yes, it's a human voice

maybe always been

a delicate, hissing voice

a little snarling dreamworks'
funko satan for kids

who reviews the predicament of
his babies:

no más; no mass shootings

everybody inside? wes craven's
weekend at bernie's

gov. inslee calls me out for going outside barefoot

we're eating our fingers listening to television;
follow me for more self-deprecating recipes,
including:

banging your head against the wall,
mean butterfly effects,
&& checking in on people who couldn't

care less what the void is saying back to you

i'm sorry, but when i heard 'social
distancing' i thought you meant

temporarily

how is life on the new obverse

are you surviving unprecedented levels of
fomo, reminisced;

swatting away thoughts of an alternate
frame of consciousness where you might exist,

now, as a hideously disfigured,
idiot circus ?

every day you're spittin'
a sloth recital,

and, now, you're not sure,
you're really not sure,

if your nose is even crooked
or if you'll ever confirm this

with the hazmat suits you observe
from your bell tower;

snacking on food combos
w/ threatening auras

mandarin & mayo

wasting the soft moon on absurdity

coronavirus catfish might be fucking liver failure
after all this is said and done

danny mcbride sics his sex toy gimp
channing tatum,

eating my face in the presence of god,
eating popcorn, providing the laugh-track

for our netflix special's empty stadium
for not taking covfefe seriously enough—

future trump hacked the twitter
& tried to warn us about the covid, baby

anything could be true
at this point

when the water sounds are up to our ears
& the ducks quack in approval

diaries for everyone

we carry different oceans in our eyes   living the cave dwelling moment on this shore
of memories stirring beneath the floorboards of this dive bar's smoking patio

anthropomorphic, these hindsights flex a shape and presence of their own   i'm aware
          of a history here, summoned like candy man /

          chanticleer

reconvene we must w/ simpler times; simpler times, as in a week prior
                                                            to pandemic in the usa

insatiability's author slit his wrists on acid when the germans invaded poland

we smoke as paramedics load a patient onto the ambulance outside a music venue, our exits

stumble—bernard sumner's voice is unmistakable; distracting, even, in
                                                            decision-making throes

will it be shells made of mozzarella with ground beef cooked in duck
          fat tossed in curry catsup,
or will it be a stockpile of frozen munchies?

whole foods is not a cost effective option during a pandemic   i assure
you my shopping here is purely circumstantial

i was leaving comcast as i had been pandemically enforced
to purchase a modem to begin telecommuting from home

so there i was mid peruse big o' hungry eyes like mama used to make

when the wife suggests we get serious
about canned cuisines   it gets the heart a fluttering you know

because there are two wolves inside me: one wolf is the wolf from the three little piggies
and he's here for the slop since it can be a tasty challenge to elevate

the other wolf is the wolf from little red riding hood impersonating grandma,
acting very frugal about the price of provisions at this particular establishment

this is my wheel-less road i must travel as over time we begin to callous the soles
of our personal economies to the expense of inconvenience
so just push through and vote for the former wolf and go to town best we can

we're at check-out and the cashier asks if we have an amazon prime account
          (deduct a percentage) and it takes us three minutes to figure out how to process
     such a request   such a pressurizing request with the line behind us sweating us out and
     when it finally processes we save a whopping bopping thirty-seven cents

tumbleweeds trip me in the office

it's funny that i'm troubleshooting how to install a proper workstation at home
so i can be safe from the virus while i'm the only one in the office

i'm just glad they left the lights on and the sun is coming through the windows

at least the sweet and kind receptionists are still here they even complimented me on my
haircut and i told 'em it was to look nice for corona   we live in the same moment
so we shared a laugh

          employees of the service industry united to educate the public   they are without
health insurance or sick leave at their prospective jobs and this should be a   thoroughly
addressed talking point to decrease the spread of the virus   unfortunately the public
responded by showing less attendance at their local watering holes, creating an
entirely new monster by the name of rent

there's actually a third wolf inside me and it's tex avery's zoot suit
                                                                 wolf

          obsessed with corey feldman's documentary about the child molestation he and
corey haim endured

soda pop clubs for teens   what american teenager wasn't a fan of the
coreys, sugary drinks, and trying to black out their own sexual abuse ? whether his intent
is pure or feldman is truly hoaxing his followers and turning a profit by exploiting his
deceased friend ('s story), some of it is true some of it is always true

          a dick tracy character who might as well be gilbert gottfried or pete davidson's
impression of a staten island guy, is on the bus begging womxn to get off with him

and have a cheeseburger in paradise he says the worst thing that could happen is sex, before this

he was doing a gleeful curbside spin preaching about love and the sun + what we should be thankful for and offered to help this disabled veteran off the bus

the disabled veteran cut him down with some good o' cussery saying

i don't touch your car so don't touch my wheelchair motherfucker motherfucker get away

　　　motherfucker, and if that isn't the concentrated spice of life what is

sebi's is my jam   it's this little polish restaurant in the eastlake neighborhood i live directly across the street from they allowed me to host an awkward poetry reading there once because i'm there quite a bit but have been going less often due to pandementia + the embarrassing uncertainty regarding my own behavior   like just because i want to make people laugh and think i'm funny doesn't mean i can afford to act as the shitty stand-up bros in chicago do which i don't think i do but hey we can't always be as self-aware as we pretend to be online

　　　i wanna show my support and gratitude as a customer and sit in my customer seat and make small talk a spicy hit of socializing you can put in my veins only who knows how far this shit is going to go

talk at the counter spills into: even canadian moguls are losing money /

　　　every time i cough i'm afraid a tranquilizer is gonna stick me in my neck and a net is gonna drop on me

the worst so far hasn't even happened yet but yo at least i can say

greetings from the bunker

peter pan is taking a bath

tinker bell massages the shampoo into a foam

peter smashes action figures of captain hook and tick-tock

vacant boathouses in russia

respirators collect in the gutters

like random ugg boots and panties

center justify
the uncomfortable music
cards against manatees
who aren't fucking around
to find out
if you will burn it down, child

they're fully versed
in what you're capable of